Quebec Passages

by Pearl Pirie

Pearl Pirie (1972-)
© 2014, Noun Trivet Press, Canada
ISBN: 978-0-9878663-3-2

an hour and a half into the forests of Quebec

"so greenly history puts forth thorns"
~ Eve Luckring

try to do the math of a hillside –
count the maples, birches and pines
on any square yard. work out
some guesstimate of length.

how many individual plants?
it sums to some forgiveness

which comes in softer lines
for the settlers who slashed
milled or burned all that they saw
as theirs, as if trees were infinite.

back on our cement block, news:
Nestlé is one of a few multinationals

who pump a small lake a year into this
crinkle-squeeze plastic convenience
accommodating a lack of planning.
as if aquifers were for me alone.

as if our block didn't use that much
alone each with our hose on the lawn.

as a traveling companion

the blank page
could do better

sure, it flatteringly
wants to let me
talk about me

but discloses
not a half-note
about itself

at the edge of landscape's privacy

5

what I'm missing

not a drunk, *with many a sniggering jest.*
for hours I haven't been asked

for change, bus tickets, a smile. no
crack-heads no off-meds. shoulders soften.

not a single child with an ear-infection
nor cat pleading utterly cruelly starved.

not even an unanswered ring of
telemarketer. have we outrun the food chain?

are we suspended mid-air. don't look down.
don't open your eyes. feign grade 2 sick day sleep.

in quiet like this one could believe
in omens. or be susceptible to beauty.

ensconced in a bucket seat,

being present is the ultimate in ephemerals. one mood opens
all the rooms to that mood.

explore. behind that shelter there was a movement, a mound
of curious rounded rectangle

with an improbably thin tail which zig zags as if on an eroding
scent, chasing vapours.

see how it takes a dive at the snow. a second time, hits crust. a third time
he is in past his shoulder.

does he grunt the smallest ufffs bit by bit, in-ner, all in but the
oh, and all in.

people who almost miss a beat of their strides would never distinguish his dip
in snow from the general surface

uneven, blown, drifted, in night.

staring in the slanting snow with the flag pole's soft clang
of rope, as pines shrug.

the gusts shift weight to my toes but mole shrew vole or
whatever name for grey pelted

he doesn't leave his warm cover. I am inside my travel, carriage, book,
words, head, away from hawks.

2 hours and 17 minutes

into this ride and someone
in this car could not abide
the heat—releases sweaty
socks for us all to share.
may as well be over
all our noses, elephantine
sway the trumpets.

flower lover

lower love flow over flover-loo ow low love, er
the y in *very* missing & the sideways *u* to make
flower a bird, a plover is missing, plow missing
who has stolen what isn't there? the power &
the elloo & the oweb & the stammer of liquid
l, the way r stops short before making a gerund
of itself, of us all. maybe we all are noun-verbs.

F L O W E R

thirst of the mouth breathers, or
to live like a dracaena

in lack of water, it does not die.
it pares itself. what is oldest it sucks
to a dry husk, taking back much

of what it gave, drops the lowest
leaves as mulch to keep in
what moisture it can retain.

where is my oldest self that I can
dispense with? these thick ankles
like camel's double humps misplaced?

the dracaena keeps growing, slower,
with fewer leaves, enough to keep
sun but less to maintain. it waits

like an old man on poor land, waiting
with the poor of the land for luck to
change. but the poor have feet to march.

the quickness

travel reduces us to the excretory
feeding tubes that we are. baby
birds, all of us. dim, too dim to see.

give me a flashlight to glow the pink
stretch between the translucent
beaks of books. will mother return?

should the food cart not return,
should it return empty except for
the sound of its one squeaky wheel,

we can't choke down its good for nothing
hollow comfort. we need our fecal sacs
carried away. would brass-badged refuse?

hair strokes

"things recede, everything recedes, everything is far away
[...] the moon of contemplation on our backs"
~ Tim Lilburn, Moosewood Sandhills

from every angle examined, yep, still 2 white hairs

as a teen you said: I want to love you till we're grey
we're there,...

no, the whole head, and if you go bald. then too.

twenty years. you're still here, your hand thrust into my side,
rooting for a grip to hang on.

after the meltdown at Promenade Plantée where shoppers and
suits averted their already preoccupied gaze we returned to
our flophouse de jour

waking to sun,
your hand on my back
was feeling a vertebra
as if testing for
a weak rung

general boarding

she spreads out a paper camp
tilts her seat back, hits the knees behind,

feels the reflexive Canadian social seatbelt tug;
she does the customary suck-breath-wince

it's too quiet in here for her to speak
she mouths "sorry". if she could

her neck would fly into a thousand cranes,
become a murmuration of Saraswati's smile.

rain taps

we still believe in birds. can't see wings.
in fields, islands of forests

a mean time, stuck here
with & without wifi, & with i.

frost-thrown crop of stones
collected on the hay wagon

a chicken wire corn crib;
how does my brain name it?

a bird I understand is swallow,
before word in or out

maybe this weekend
celibacy will be belayed

rain washes persistently
finds the clay under the topsoil

stretch, wiggle hands
but the right is locked in sleep

cocker spaniel ears totter
a joy loop to train, train, train,

moss is a velvet cape laid down

welcome back milkweed, lamb's ears,
grapevine and smallest of clover sprout.
good to see you up and about. apple petal.

verdigris pixie cup. dark umbrella lobbed
into the bush's sand, broken and turned
back on itself. oh, hello, rosette of lobes,

tar jelly lichen. what we saw once up close
we can draw in details from a distance.
we know a smudge is weather.

we breathe and know rain's close. we have
no word for the taste of air but know a shift
once our bones feel it. we notice best what

we have an easy word for. what we might
even believe. or else we're stranded in hail
in diagonal sweeps of musical sheets.

a country untouched

by civil war on our soil we are the peacekeepers except for Oka, and squirmishes and wars before the Iroquois Confederacy and deportation from Acadie and and forced relocation to English homes of natives and the children from Ireland made into slaves and 2012 with twenty-three people shot on Danzig in east Scarborough and fourteen who died in 1989 at École Polytechnique. and police reported 121 incidents of impaired driving causing death in 2011, and the small violences of shortened longevity by tetanus 2005-2011 is 3 so forget that, measles 750 in 2011 but no death, unnecessary grief, what else for the fret machinery? Smoking is responsible for 16.6 per cent of all deaths in Canada. but

we are a country of peace. we give aid. we train doctors. we take in refugees, except for those we turn away Komagata Maru, and the M.S. St. Louis 1938, and new standards to promote the English- and French-speaking and trained to then refuse to let them transition to their field we are a peaceful people.

what are we protecting with the Department of National Defense? the largest federal government department with over 110,000 employees, including 65,000 Regular Force members, 25,000 Reserve Force members and 28,000 civilians. DND and the Canadian Forces together have a budget of approximately 18 billion dollars, but arts sector has them outnumbered with 140,000 authors, actor, comedians, singers visual artists and if we include cultural workers of architects and bookstore workers, and the important etc we're 609,000. But who will feed us all? 293,925 farmers. percentage falling.

mer Experience Representat...

ꓸꓸꓸons

Styles ▾ ≣

ꓸ0 ꓸ2

I just noticed that it i

National I Hate Mys
(which means the ne
and want to live fore
for a cold night in Bo

and all afternoon. Tl
tomorrow will be jus
only different. I'm in
at the edge of town, l

A sparrow limps past
I am Frederico García Lorca
risen from the dead–
literature will lose, sunlight wi

Franz Wright

Government and Military

Job Type
- Full Time
- Employee

and we are all us --
and it can drag us all down to sympathetic grief

it could restart the cascades. stiff upper...
let us stay up here

rabbits, cl
whiskers e
but aren't

when out
when ami
who woul
unless at

when a fri
what her
-- a woma
sees a rabl
folds a ges
I cut her o
her mothe
and langu

Untitled 2

```
intellectual 3
philosophical 8        differential 1           smaller 3
self-defeating 1
identitarian 2                   communitarian 1 egotist 2
determinate 1
object-oriented 1              concrete 1              p
contextualized 2
pseudouniversalist 1           linguistic 8           c
        human 25
Marxian 1      possible 8      abject 3              t
technological 5
Solid 5         natural 10     objective 3          e
        collective 8
Unusual 2       astonishing 3  authorial 1          u
        meaningless 1
Democratic 1    inescapable 2  false 2              c
        newer 1
Tolerant 1      higher 3       rightful 1           j
        dystopian 3
Risky 1 civil 1        twentieth 7          anonymous
freeing 1
Presidential 1  weekly 1       non-profit 1         f
        queer 1
Trans 1 telepathic 1   confident 1          courageou
outspoken 1
Collaged 3      hand-painted 1                       d
        incredible 3
Untitled 3      Egyptian 1     touring 2            e
        packed 2
```

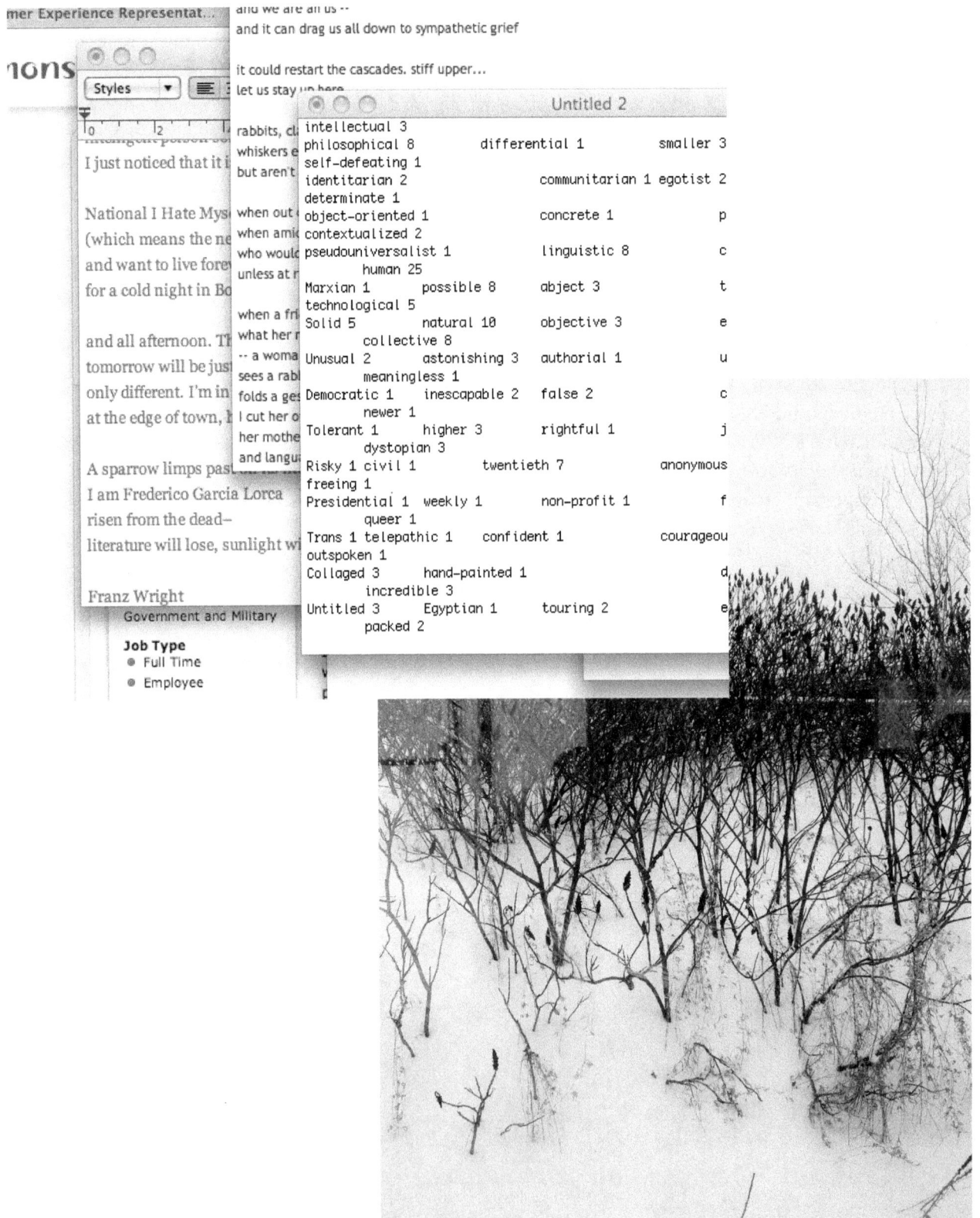

glass–scapes

past his lap
and a blurred forespin

a stubble rub heat
on my face from nuzzle

the hum of cornfields
the ho of sun or rain

Somali call the weather
devil beating his wife

some cloud or another
is cotton-eyed

remembering transport

the form has a fringe
widening like wings

a spinning Möbius strip of the
ponchoed lovers who kiss

a diagonal wind brings
snow to their wool

a star-field falls on
their felted berets

their shoulders
are stitched

in black and blonde
dreadlocks, a westward drift.

they stop again,
the train comes, goes.

what fool would end that
or even pause

for something as pedestrian
as diesel transport.

as a tourist passing a train station

peculiar the things I know
in language that I can't hear.

apology tumbles toward her face.
his few words stumble out,

words staggering, his hand clutches
the doorframe of his mouth in surprise,

his suspicion flashes. he settles on
a guttural, his breath rises for more.

steadies and studies himself, a determined
clench of all relevant muscles

(and perhaps some that weren't)
while a few went astray. (twitch.)

straightened against the silence
of drizzle: one, two hard squints

at the rain beyond his head as tho to
chin bump *hey* to the air.

to fall in love through the ear

or through the eyes is to go thru
a very small aperture

to slip in under the skin,
for a filarial worm, living is loving
is backwashing from the kiss
of mosquitoes into a person
or from someone's
sticky swamp of blood
where one is the nursery
into the mosquito's maw.

how you enter
is a way to say love
what you intend
makes all the difference.

an estuary of sea birds

an outcrop of rock island.
so, the stomach is that stone

the heart is cedar and
thoughts are gull-intelligent

each turns for its own
shifts of overlapping calls

outnumbering the two crows
on the neuron of an elm

water, depths, shadows, waves
cancel each other.

to bite back the travel bug is to be a woman kicking back at a gelding

i. June

you have to respect that a horse is bigger than you are.
June, June, tell him you're there, that you're coming.
don't be mauling around him when he's in mood
not like that. let him simmer down a while.
where would you be if he kicked you?

I'd get up and kick him right back.
twice as hard and he'd learn
we're equals. he won't lord me.

no, you'd be dead, June, dead.
or liable to be.

June drove a tall van
with a roadrunner decal.
big, seated high up, so people
can see her coming and get out of her way
this time she's not going to be the one to move.

ii. this will make her think twice

father lifted the foal
her newborn legs scattered
her eyes twisting white,
searching for ground. my father sure
this submission to greater fates
is the first essential lesson.

when she is 1100 pounds
and 14 hands high, she'll think
he can still, on whim, lift her
and just chooses not to.

you have to instill that fear
he said, or they'll turn on you
without thinking twice.

iii larger than me, this muscle of journey

picking it up
and setting it down
when this trip
was as small as a book.

it didn't learn
that I am the master.

even before we began
it had its own rigid spine.

it said then, quieter than now, ride me
as you can, but I am more feral
than you think you are.

there's no master here.

a field of Quebec sumac

is a Somalian savanna
to someone homesick enough.
to someone needing a sign it's enough
hope to keep posterity alive.

memory is as close we can muster.
touch it, as if it were the name of G_d
the ink on every card ever signed
from father with his own hand.

power

with the wires
to the horizon
it runs upwards

see it? lift your eyes
up that gap between
evening-black trees.

a rail–bed of feldspar

mirage: my cousin whispering the meaning of slag,
us collecting the black shine of what trains burned

he purported to know train schedules. (did he?)
that day, yes. behind thin branches my cousin and I

cedar's sweet fingers is not exactly an armor
against metal or stones or authorities

the conductor probably saw our orange corduroys
or else our red Montreal Canadiens baseball caps

or remembered that we waved to him most Sundays
from that near wigwag, but we followed

the rules we set for ourselves (what more
can we ask?) retreated to the safe distance

where the pennies we laid on the sun-glinted track
would not hit us with their pink ovals, shiny, renewed.

a surrogate her is outside

i
each stem is in its ant mound.
in her parched sand garden
wilting wide-spaced plants
as that woman hangs her wash.

her sagging line, the parallel pencil line
of road. she'd be a ghost by now
(is that the polite way to put it?)
the shush of coat & tarred sleepers.

ii
20 years ago that wife's scarecrow
the tattered overalls in wind

how I panged then for dad
the first nostalgia since I left

iii
overhear how my cousin said it,
"your dad is timeless"
everything comes back
to him. every summer day:

damp straw hat, red and white
polka dot handkerchief, overalls,
feet kettle-stoned with heat
propped in twiggy grass,

workboots off, blackflies on,
a lawn chair under basswood

the basswood cut, lawn chair broke
all of him and his clothes pitched.

the summer day comes back
as if the muggy heat misses him.

time is space

away from home where the train whistle blows past a stalk of heron, a hug digitally given and received in real time 6 time zones apart.

as part of Rosemary's negotiation of their mortality, Andrew is moving to hospice care. the swinging doors of eras hit us when we least expect it.

her thoughts cast shore onto continents of air, into the train carriage, among Issa's Mon Annee de printemps.

Issa is no less immediate for dislocating in time or rerouting thru France. *imitant les cormorans/ les enfants / les surpassent*

there are rain puddles instead of snow melts here. a rainbow of trees yellow orange white pink lime wonder blue sky warmth of hand on my thigh.

almost Kingston and I could drowse from overstimulation of trying to pour a whole space time continuum thru 2 wide pupils or worse, words.

brown eyes, his red chestnut hers with flecks of green she with yellow hazelnut he with a blue cast as overcast over mudlake cattails.

to say brown is to say mud is clay is sand is something common, as if common ever feels common, or could hold mundane for a minute.

becoming an edible woman

menthol passes thru the carriage

a masseuse, the train rocks me centred
its palm rolling my hard boiled shell

left, right, until it peels off what isn't
essentially me, not anymore

maybe she will wake

her head thrown back again,
giggles pealed like grapes —

she hasn't slapped up aisle
for a while. maybe napping.

before her destination
all the little sandals sleep.

References for *A Country Untouched*:

Canada in Crisis (2): An Agenda for Survival of the Nation by Robert A. Battram

http://en.wikipedia.org/wiki/List_of_countries_by_GDP_(PPP)

http://ccrweb.ca/canadarefugeeshistory6.htm

arts sector: http://www.canadacouncil.ca/en/council/resources/arts-promotion/arts-promo-kit/part1

http://www.phac-aspc.gc.ca/im/vpd-mev/measles-rougeole-eng.php

Impaired driving in Canada, http://www.statcan.gc.ca/pub/85-002-x/2013001/article/11739-eng.htm

http://www.rcinet.ca/en/2013/05/31/smoking-tobacco-still-a-leading-cause-of-death-in-canada/

farmers: http://www.statcan.gc.ca/daily-quotidien/120510/dq120510a-eng.htm

Thanks to Max Middle for producing a broadsheet with "at the edge of landscape's privacy". Thanks to Stuart Ross and Daphne Marlatt who read earlier versions of the manuscripts this has been and who said encouraging and useful things. Thanks to Jean Van Loon and to Michael Dennis for reading, commenting and encouraging.

Thanks to all the audiences who heard test runs of these poems over the last few years and the folks at Poetry-W who lent their eyes to show what wasn't clear.

Thanks to The Rubies for pressure on clarity and to the sound and vispo makers for their open doors.

Thanks to hubby who risks "do you want to hear a poem" each time he passes through a room.

Thanks to VIA Rail for making comfy seats and quiet rides.

www.ingramcontent.com/pod-product-compliance
Lightning Source LLC
LaVergne TN
LVHW081323060426
835509LV00015B/1648